DIABETIC RECIPES

FOR THE HOLIDAYS

FACTS ABOUT DIABETES

Low-calorie, low-fat, low-cholesterol and low-sodium—buzzwords of the decade and for a good reason. People today are more aware than ever before of the roles that diet and exercise play in maintaining a healthful lifestyle. For people with diabetes and their families, the positive impact good nutrition and physical activity have on well-being is very familiar.

Diabetes is a disease that affects the body's ability to use glucose as a source of fuel. When glucose is utilized improperly, it can build up in the bloodstream, creating higher than normal blood sugar levels. Left unchecked, elevated blood sugar levels may lead to the development of more serious long-term complications like blindness and heart and kidney disease.

Not all cases of diabetes are alike. In fact, the disease presents itself in two very distinct forms—Type I and Type II. Development of diabetes during childhood or adolescence is typical of Type I, or juvenile-onset, diabetes. These individuals are unable to make insulin, a hormone produced by the pancreas that moves glucose from the bloodstream into the body's cells, where it is used as a source of fuel. Daily injections of insulin, coupled with a balanced meal plan, are the focus of treatment.

People who develop Type II diabetes, the more common form of the disease, are typically over the age of 40 and obese. These individuals produce insulin but the amount is insufficient to meet their needs, or their excess weight renders the hormone incapable of adequately performing its functions. Treatment includes balanced eating, moderate weight loss, exercise and, in extreme cases, oral hypoglycemic agents or insulin injections.

Maximize Health, Minimize Complications

Diabetes increases one's risk of developing high blood pressure and high blood cholesterol levels. Over time, elevated levels may progress to more serious complications, including heart and kidney disease, stroke and hypertension. In fact, research shows that individuals with diabetes are nineteen times more likely to develop kidney disease and four times more likely to suffer from heart disease or a stroke than people who do not have diabetes. While heredity plays a major role in the development of these complications, regular check-ups with your physician and registered dietitian to fine-tune treatment strategies are good ways to help minimize complications. Strategies for treatment vary among individuals, yet overall goals remain the same: achieving and maintaining near-normal blood sugar levels by balancing food intake, insulin and activity; achieving optimal blood cholesterol levels; and improving overall health through good nutrition.

Balance Is the Key

Achieving optimal nutrition often requires lifestyle changes to balance the intake of nutrients. The United States Department of Agriculture and the United States Department of Health and Human Services developed the Dietary Guidelines to simplify the basics of balanced eating and to help all individuals develop healthful eating plans. Several of the guidelines follow but were adjusted to include the revised 1994 American Diabetes Association's Nutrition Recommendations. Because recommendations are broad, work with your physician and registered dietitian to personalize the guidelines to meet your specific needs.

Eat a variety of foods. Energy, protein, vitamins, minerals and fiber are essential for optimal health, but no one food contains them all. Including a wide range of foods in your diet and using fats and oils sparingly throughout the day are easy ways to consume all the nutrients your body needs. Carbohydrate should comprise between 45 and 55 percent of total calories, and protein should contribute between 10 and 20 percent.

Maintain a healthy weight. Excess weight can worsen your diabetes and encourages the development of more severe complications. Research shows that shedding 10 to 20 pounds is enough to initiate positive results for obese individuals. Combining a healthful eating plan with physical activity outlined by your health care team is the best medicine for maintaining a healthy weight.

Choose a diet low in fat, saturated fat and cholesterol. Fat has more than double the calories of an equal amount of protein or carbohydrate. Thus, diets low in fat make it easier to maintain a desirable weight and decrease the likelihood of developing high blood cholesterol levels. Limit fat to no more than 30 percent of total calories, saturated fat to no more than 10 percent of total calories and daily cholesterol to no more than 300 mg. The 30 percent of calories from fat goal applies to a total diet over time, not to a single food, serving of a recipe or meal.

Choose a diet with plenty of vegetables, fruits and grain products.
Vitamins, minerals, fiber and complex carbohydrates abound in these
low-fat food choices. Filling up on fiber leaves less room for fat and may
produce a slight decrease in blood cholesterol levels. Antioxidants such
as beta carotene and the vitamins C and E may protect against heart
disease, while magnesium, phosphorous and calcium are minerals that
may keep blood pressure levels under control.

Use sugars in moderation. The ban on sugar has been lifted for people
with diabetes but it is not altogether gone. The new guidelines for simple
sugar intake are based on scientific research that indicates that
carbohydrate in the form of simple sugars does not raise blood sugar
levels more rapidly than any other type of carbohydrate food. What is
more important is the total amount of carbohydrate consumed, not the
source. However, keep in mind that since simple sugars are loaded with
calories, contain no vitamins and minerals, and are linked to the
development of cavities, it is still a good idea to limit your intake of
simple sugars to no more than 25 percent of total carbohydrate.

Use salt and sodium in moderation. Some people with diabetes may be
more sensitive to sodium than others, making them more susceptible to
high blood pressure. Minimize this risk by limiting sodium intake to no
more than 2,400 mg a day (about 1 teaspoon of salt) and choosing single
food items with less than 400 mg of sodium and entrées with less than
800 mg of sodium per serving.

Facts About the Food

The recipes in this publication were designed with people with diabetes
in mind. But all are based on the principles of sound nutrition as
outlined by the Dietary Guidelines, making them perfect for the entire
family. Though the recipes in this publication are not intended as a
medically therapeutic program, nor as a substitute for medically
approved meal plans for individuals with diabetes, they are low in
calories, fat, sodium and cholesterol and will fit easily into an
individualized meal plan designed by your physician, registered dietitian
and you.

Facts About the Exchanges

The nutrition information that appears with each recipe was calculated by an independent nutrition consulting firm, and the Dietary Exchanges are based on the Exchange Lists for Meal Planning developed by American Diabetes Association/The American Dietetic Association. Every effort has been made to check the accuracy of these numbers. However, because numerous variables account for a wide range of values in certain foods, all analyses that appear in this book should be considered approximate.

■ The analysis of each recipe includes all the ingredients that are listed in that recipe, *except* ingredients labeled as "optional" or "for garnish." Nutritional analysis is provided for the primary recipe only, not for the recipe variations.

■ If a range is offered for an ingredient, the *first* amount given was used to calculate the nutrition information.

■ If an ingredient is presented with an option ("2 cups hot cooked rice or noodles," for example), the *first* item listed was used to calculate the nutrition information.

■ Foods shown in photographs on the same serving plate and offered as "serve with" suggestions at the end of a recipe are *not* included in the recipe analysis unless they are listed in the ingredient list.

■ Meat should be trimmed of all visible fat because this is reflected in the nutritional analysis.

■ In recipes calling for cooked rice or noodles, the analysis was based on rice or noodles that were prepared without added salt and fat.

■ Most processed foods contain a significant amount of sodium and the amount of sodium is reflected in the analysis. Rinsing canned or jarred processed foods such as beans and tuna under cold running water for one minute eliminates between 40 and 60 percent of added sodium.

SPICY VEGETABLE QUESADILLAS

These Southwestern treats are the perfect starters for any party or family gathering. Full of flavor and spice, no one will suspect they're so low in fat.

Nonstick cooking spray
1 small zucchini, chopped
½ cup chopped green bell pepper
½ cup chopped onion
2 cloves garlic, minced
½ teaspoon ground cumin
½ teaspoon chili powder
8 (6-inch) flour tortillas
1 cup (4 ounces) shredded reduced-fat Cheddar cheese
¼ cup chopped fresh cilantro

1 Spray large nonstick skillet with cooking spray. Heat over medium heat until hot. Add zucchini, pepper, onion, garlic, cumin and chili powder; cook and stir 3 to 4 minutes or until vegetables are crisp-tender. Remove vegetable mixture and set aside; wipe skillet clean.

2 Spoon vegetable mixture evenly over half of each tortilla. Sprinkle each evenly with cheese and cilantro. Fold each tortilla in half.

3 Spray same skillet with cooking spray. Add tortillas and heat 1 to 2 minutes per side over medium heat or until lightly browned. Cut into thirds before serving.

Makes 8 servings

Nutrients per Serving:

Calories	153 (22% calories from fat)				
Total Fat	4 g	Carbohydrate	23 g	Iron	trace
Saturated Fat	1 g	Dietary Fiber	1 g	Vitamin A	56 RE
Cholesterol	8 mg	Protein	7 g	Vitamin C	15 mg
Sodium	201 mg	Calcium	112 mg	Sugar	1 g

DIETARY EXCHANGES: 1½ Starch/Bread, ½ Lean Meat, ½ Fat

SMOKED SALMON APPETIZERS

Turn the classic combination of lox, bagels and cream cheese into an elegant opening for your holiday festivities. Lox is smoked salmon that has been brine-cured before smoking, resulting in a saltier taste; if you wish, ask for the less salty "Nova" lox.

¼ cup reduced-fat or fat-free
 cream cheese, softened
1 tablespoon chopped fresh dill
 or 1 teaspoon dried dill
 weed

⅛ teaspoon ground red pepper
4 ounces thinly sliced smoked
 salmon or lox
24 melba toast rounds or other
 low-fat crackers

1 Combine cream cheese, dill and pepper in small bowl; stir to blend. Spread evenly over each slice of salmon. Starting with short side, roll up salmon slices jelly-roll fashion. Place on plate; cover with plastic wrap. Chill at least 1 hour or up to 4 hours before serving.

2 Using a sharp knife, cut salmon rolls crosswise into ¾-inch pieces. Place pieces, cut side down, on serving plate. Garnish each piece with dill sprig, if desired. Serve cold or at room temperature with melba rounds.

Makes about 2 dozen appetizers
(3 appetizers per serving)

Nutrients per Serving:

Calories	80 (21% calories from fat)					
Total Fat	2 g	Carbohydrate	10 g	Iron	trace
Saturated Fat	1 g	Dietary Fiber	1 g	Vitamin A	36 RE
Cholesterol	6 mg	Protein	6 g	Vitamin C	trace
Sodium	241 mg	Calcium	27 mg	Sugar	0 g

DIETARY EXCHANGES: ½ Starch/Bread, ½ Lean Meat

SHRIMP DIP WITH CRUDITÉS

Any combination of raw vegetables, including broccoli, cauliflower or celery, can be added to this simple, yet elegant appetizer. Be sure to choose veggies of different colors and shapes to create an eye-catching display.

1 can (6 ounces) cooked
    shrimp, drained, divided
½ cup reduced-fat cream
    cheese, softened
⅓ cup plus 1 tablespoon thinly
    sliced green onions, divided
3 tablespoons light or fat-free
    Caesar salad dressing
2 teaspoons prepared
    horseradish

¼ teaspoon salt
2 red or yellow bell peppers,
    cut into 2×1-inch pieces
4 large carrots, peeled,
    diagonally sliced ¼ inch
    thick
10 crispbread or other low-fat
    crackers

1 Reserve several shrimp for garnish. Combine remaining shrimp, cream cheese, ⅓ cup green onions, salad dressing, horseradish and salt in medium bowl; mix well. Transfer to serving dish; top with reserved shrimp and remaining 1 tablespoon green onions. Cover and chill at least 30 minutes before serving.

2 Serve with bell peppers, carrots and crackers. *Makes 10 servings*

Nutrients per Serving:

Calories	127 (29% calories from fat)				
Total Fat	4 g	Carbohydrate	16 g	Iron	1 mg
Saturated Fat	trace	Dietary Fiber	2 g	Vitamin A	1133 RE
Cholesterol	37 mg	Protein	7 g	Vitamin C	106 mg
Sodium	217 mg	Calcium	41 mg	Sugar	2 g

DIETARY EXCHANGES: ½ Starch/Bread, ½ Lean Meat, 2 Vegetable, ½ Fat

OREGON HOT APPLE CIDER

To warm up those cold holiday nights, sit by the fire and sip this enticing classic direct from the Pacific Northwest. The pear provides an elegant touch.

8 whole cloves
8 cups apple cider
½ cup dried cherries
½ cup dried cranberries

3 cinnamon sticks, broken in
  half
1 pear, quartered, cored, sliced

1 Bundle cloves in small piece of cheesecloth. Tie cheesecloth to form small sack.

2 Combine cider, cherries, cranberries, cinnamon and cheesecloth sack in large saucepan. Heat just to a simmer; do not boil. Remove cheesecloth sack and discard.

3 Add pear before serving.   *Makes 8 servings*

Nutrients per Serving:

Calories	180 (3% calories from fat)					
Total Fat	1 g	Carbohydrate	48 g	Iron	2 mg
Saturated Fat	trace	Dietary Fiber	2 g	Vitamin A	97 RE
Cholesterol	0 mg	Protein	1 g	Vitamin C	13 mg
Sodium	10 mg	Calcium	31 mg	Sugar	2 g

DIETARY EXCHANGES: 3 Fruit

❖

Cook's Tip

To quickly ripen a pear, place it, along with an apple, in a paper bag. Poke a few holes in the bag with a knife and let the bag stand at room temperature.

❖

SPICY PUMPKIN SOUP WITH GREEN CHILI SWIRL

Warm up the winter holidays with this Southwestern special featuring regional spices and the added kick of green chilies. Chilies may be rinsed in cold water before using to decrease spiciness.

1 can (4 ounces) diced green chilies, drained
¼ cup reduced-fat sour cream
¼ cup fresh cilantro leaves
1 can (15 ounces) solid-pack pumpkin
1 can (about 14 ounces) fat-free reduced-sodium chicken broth

½ cup water
1 teaspoon ground cumin
½ teaspoon chili powder
¼ teaspoon garlic powder
⅛ teaspoon ground red pepper (optional)

1 Combine green chilies, sour cream and cilantro in food processor or blender; process until smooth.*

2 Combine pumpkin, chicken broth, water, cumin, chili powder, garlic powder and pepper, if desired, in medium saucepan; stir in ¼ cup green chili mixture. Bring to a boil; reduce heat to medium. Simmer, uncovered, 5 minutes, stirring occasionally.

3 Pour into serving bowls. Top each serving with small dollops of remaining green chili mixture and additional sour cream, if desired. Run tip of spoon through dollops to swirl.   *Makes 4 servings*

*Omit food processor step by adding green chilies directly to soup. Finely chop cilantro and combine with sour cream. Dollop with sour cream mixture as directed.

Nutrients per Serving:

Calories	72 (17% calories from fat)				
Total Fat	1 g	Carbohydrate	12 g	Iron	2 mg
Saturated Fat	trace	Dietary Fiber	4 g	Vitamin A	2424 RE
Cholesterol	5 mg	Protein	4 g	Vitamin C	5 mg
Sodium	276 mg	Calcium	57 mg	Sugar	0 g

DIETARY EXCHANGES: 1 Starch/Bread

TEXAS-STYLE CHILI

Called a "bowl of red" deep in the heart of Texas, this chili is usually served with the beans on the side. For those who like their chili with a bit more fire, use a hotter salsa or even a few dashes of hot pepper sauce. This dish is even better when it's prepared a day ahead, chilled and brought back to a simmer before serving.

Nonstick cooking spray
1 pound lean boneless beef chuck, cut into ½-inch pieces
2 cups chopped onions
5 cloves garlic, minced
2 tablespoons chili powder
1 tablespoon ground cumin
1 teaspoon ground coriander
1 teaspoon dried oregano leaves or ground oregano

2½ cups fat-free reduced-sodium beef broth
1 cup prepared salsa or picante sauce
2 cans (16 ounces each) pinto or red beans (or one of each), rinsed and drained
½ cup chopped fresh cilantro
½ cup nonfat sour cream
1 cup chopped ripe tomatoes

1 Spray Dutch oven or large saucepan with nonstick cooking spray; heat over medium-high heat until hot. Add beef, onions and garlic; cook and stir until beef is no longer pink, about 5 minutes. Sprinkle mixture with chili powder, cumin, coriander and oregano; mix well. Add beef broth and salsa; bring to a boil. Cover; simmer 45 minutes.

2 Stir in beans; continue to simmer uncovered 30 minutes or until beef is tender and chili has thickened, stirring occasionally.

3 Stir in cilantro. Ladle into bowls; top with sour cream and tomatoes. Garnish with pickled jalapeño peppers, if desired.   *Makes 8 servings*

Nutrients per Serving:

Calories	268 (21% calories from fat)					
Total Fat	7 g	Carbohydrate	31 g	Iron	3 mg
Saturated Fat	2 g	Dietary Fiber	2 g	Vitamin A	194 RE
Cholesterol	37 mg	Protein	25 g	Vitamin C	21 mg
Sodium	725 mg	Calcium	62 mg	Sugar	2 g

DIETARY EXCHANGES: 1½ Starch/Bread, 2½ Lean Meat, 1 Vegetable

SANTA FE GRILLED VEGETABLE SALAD

Nothing beats the flavor of food off the grill, especially if the marinade is as robust as this citrus-enhanced Southwestern fare. You may want to peel the eggplant after grilling, as the skin may be slightly bitter.

1 medium yellow summer squash, cut into halves

1 medium zucchini, cut into halves

1 green bell pepper, cut into quarters

1 red bell pepper, cut into quarters

2 baby eggplants (6 ounces each), cut into halves

1 small onion, peeled, cut into halves

½ cup orange juice

2 tablespoons lime juice

1 tablespoon olive oil

2 cloves garlic, minced

1 teaspoon dried oregano leaves

¼ teaspoon salt

¼ teaspoon ground red pepper

¼ teaspoon ground black pepper

2 tablespoons chopped fresh cilantro

1 Combine all ingredients except cilantro in large bowl; toss to coat.

2 To prevent sticking, spray grid with nonstick cooking spray. Prepare coals for grilling. Place vegetables on grid, 2 to 3 inches from hot coals; reserve marinade. Grill 3 to 4 minutes per side or until tender and lightly charred; cool 10 minutes. Or, place vegetables on rack of broiler pan coated with nonstick cooking spray; reserve marinade. Broil 2 to 3 inches from heat, 3 to 4 minutes per side or until tender; cool 10 minutes.

3 Remove peel from eggplants, if desired. Slice vegetables into bite-sized pieces; return to reserved marinade. Stir in cilantro; toss to coat.

Makes 8 servings

Nutrients per Serving:

Calories	63 (27% calories from fat)				
Total Fat	2 g	Carbohydrate	11 g	Iron	1 mg
Saturated Fat	trace	Dietary Fiber	1 g	Vitamin A	210 RE
Cholesterol	0 mg	Protein	2 g	Vitamin C	85 mg
Sodium	70 mg	Calcium	27 mg	Sugar	2 g

DIETARY EXCHANGES: 2 Vegetable, ½ Fat

NEW ENGLAND CLAM CHOWDER

The word "chowder" comes from the French word chaudière, *the stew pot in which fishermen cooked their catches of the day. The New England version features milk, while the Manhattan (or red) variety adds tomatoes to the basic recipe.*

1 can (5 ounces) whole baby
    clams, undrained
1 baking potato, peeled,
    coarsely chopped
¼ cup finely chopped onion

⅔ cup evaporated skimmed milk
¼ teaspoon ground white pepper
¼ teaspoon dried thyme leaves
1 tablespoon reduced-calorie
    margarine

1 Drain clams; reserve juice. Add enough water to reserved juice to measure ⅔ cup. Combine clam juice mixture, potato and onion in medium saucepan. Bring to a boil over high heat; reduce heat and simmer 8 minutes or until potato is tender.

2 Add milk, pepper and thyme to saucepan. Increase heat to medium-high. Cook and stir 2 minutes. Add margarine. Cook 5 minutes or until chowder thickens, stirring occasionally.

3 Add clams; cook and stir 5 minutes or until clams are firm.

Makes 2 servings

Nutrients per Serving:

Calories	191 (18% calories from fat)				
Total Fat	4 g	Carbohydrate	27 g	Iron	4 mg
Saturated Fat	1 g	Dietary Fiber	1 g	Vitamin A	164 RE
Cholesterol	47 mg	Protein	14 g	Vitamin C	7 mg
Sodium	205 mg	Calcium	298 mg	Sugar	2 g

DIETARY EXCHANGES: 1 Starch/Bread, 1 Lean Meat, 1 Milk

SHRIMP ÉTOUFFÉE

The classic Cajun comfort food, étouffée literally means "to smother." This version eliminates most of the fat, but still "smothers" your tastebuds with abundant flavor and spice.

3 tablespoons vegetable oil
¼ cup all-purpose flour
1 cup chopped onion
1 cup chopped green bell pepper
½ cup chopped carrots
½ cup chopped celery
4 cloves garlic, minced
1 can (about 14 ounces) clear vegetable broth

1 bottle (8 ounces) clam juice
½ teaspoon salt
2½ pounds large shrimp, peeled and deveined
1 teaspoon crushed red pepper
1 teaspoon hot pepper sauce
4 cups hot cooked white or basmati rice
½ cup chopped flat leaf parsley

1 Heat oil in Dutch oven over medium heat. Add flour; cook and stir 10 to 15 minutes or until flour mixture is deep golden brown. Add onion, bell pepper, carrots, celery and garlic; cook and stir 5 minutes.

2 Stir in vegetable broth, clam juice and salt; bring to a boil. Simmer, uncovered, 10 minutes or until vegetables are tender. Stir in shrimp, red pepper and pepper sauce; simmer 6 to 8 minutes or until shrimp are opaque.

3 Ladle into eight shallow bowls; top each with ½ cup rice. Sprinkle with parsley. Serve with additional pepper sauce, if desired.

Makes 8 servings

Nutrients per Serving:

Calories	306 (20% calories from fat)				
Total Fat	7 g	Carbohydrate	32 g	Iron	5 mg
Saturated Fat	1 g	Dietary Fiber	1 g	Vitamin A	401 RE
Cholesterol	219 mg	Protein	27 g	Vitamin C	36 mg
Sodium	454 mg	Calcium	72 mg	Sugar	2 g

DIETARY EXCHANGES: 1½ Starch/Bread, 3 Lean Meat, 1 Vegetable

MUSTARD-CRUSTED ROAST PORK

3 tablespoons Dijon mustard
4 teaspoons minced garlic, divided
2 whole well-trimmed pork tenderloins, about 1 pound each
2 tablespoons dried thyme
1 teaspoon ground black pepper
½ teaspoon salt

1 pound asparagus spears, ends trimmed
2 red or yellow bell peppers (or one of each), cut lengthwise into ½-inch-wide strips
1 cup fat-free reduced-sodium chicken broth, divided

1 Preheat oven to 375°F. Combine mustard and 3 teaspoons garlic in small bowl. Spread mustard mixture evenly over top and sides of both tenderloins. Combine thyme, black pepper and salt in small bowl; reserve 1 teaspoon mixture. Sprinkle remaining mixture evenly over tenderloins, patting so that seasoning adheres to mustard. Place tenderloins on rack in shallow roasting pan. Roast 25 minutes.

2 Arrange asparagus and bell peppers in single layer in shallow casserole or 13×9-inch baking pan. Add ¼ cup broth, reserved thyme mixture and remaining 1 teaspoon garlic; toss to coat.

3 Roast vegetables in oven alongside tenderloins 15 to 20 minutes or until thermometer inserted into center of pork registers 160°F and vegetables are tender. Transfer tenderloins to carving board; tent with foil and let stand 5 minutes. Arrange vegetables on serving platter, reserving juices in dish; cover and keep warm. Add remaining ¾ cup broth and juices in dish to roasting pan. Place over range top burner(s); simmer 3 to 4 minutes over medium-high heat or until juices are reduced to ¾ cup, stirring frequently. Carve tenderloins crosswise into ¼-inch slices; arrange on serving platter. Spoon juices over pork and vegetables.

Makes 8 servings

Nutrients per Serving:

Calories	182 (23% calories from fat)					
Total Fat	5 g	Carbohydrate	8 g	Iron	4 mg
Saturated Fat	2 g	Dietary Fiber	1 g	Vitamin A	392 RE
Cholesterol	65 mg	Protein	27 g	Vitamin C	134 mg
Sodium	304 mg	Calcium	55 mg	Sugar	trace

DIETARY EXCHANGES: 3 Lean Meat, 1 Vegetable

EASY BRUNCH FRITTATA

*This Italian omelet is an ideal alternative to quiche
for your next brunch.*

1 cup small broccoli flowerets
2½ cups (12 ounces) frozen hash
    brown potatoes with onions
    and peppers (O'Brien style),
    thawed
1½ cups cholesterol-free egg
    substitute, thawed

2 tablespoons 2% low-fat milk
¾ teaspoon salt
¼ teaspoon ground black pepper
½ cup (2 ounces) shredded
    reduced-fat Cheddar cheese

1 Preheat oven to 450°F. Coat medium nonstick ovenproof skillet with nonstick cooking spray. Heat skillet over medium heat until hot. Add broccoli; cook and stir 2 minutes. Add potatoes; cook and stir 5 minutes.

2 Beat together egg substitute, milk, salt and pepper in small bowl; pour over potato mixture. Cook 5 minutes or until edges are set (center will still be wet).

3 Transfer skillet to oven; bake 6 minutes or until center is set. Sprinkle with cheese; let stand 2 to 3 minutes or until cheese is melted.

4 Cut into wedges; serve with low-fat sour cream, if desired.

Makes 6 servings

Nutrients per Serving:

Calories	102 (20% calories from fat)				
Total Fat	2 g	Carbohydrate	11 g	Iron	2 mg
Saturated Fat	1 g	Dietary Fiber	1 g	Vitamin A	135 RE
Cholesterol	7 mg	Protein	9 g	Vitamin C	23 mg
Sodium	627 mg	Calcium	124 mg	Sugar	1 g

DIETARY EXCHANGES: ½ Starch/Bread, 1 Lean Meat

SPIRITED SWEET POTATO CASSEROLE

Sweet potatoes were introduced to the South by Africans and have become synonymous with "Southern cooking." High in vitamins C and A, sweet potatoes are available year-round.

2½ pounds sweet potatoes
2 tablespoons reduced-calorie margarine
⅓ cup 1% low-fat or skim milk
¼ cup packed brown sugar
2 tablespoons bourbon or apple juice

1 teaspoon ground cinnamon
1 teaspoon vanilla
2 egg whites
½ teaspoon salt
⅓ cup chopped pecans

1 Preheat oven to 375°F. Bake potatoes 50 to 60 minutes or until very tender. Cool 10 minutes; leave oven on. Scoop pulp from warm potatoes into large bowl; discard potato skins. Add margarine to bowl; mash with potato masher until potatoes are fairly smooth and margarine has melted. Stir in milk, brown sugar, bourbon, cinnamon and vanilla; mix well.

2 Beat egg whites with electric mixer at high speed until soft peaks form. Add salt; beat until stiff peaks form. Fold egg whites into sweet potato mixture.

3 Spray 1½-quart soufflé dish with nonstick cooking spray. Spoon sweet potato mixture into dish; top with pecans.

4 Bake 30 to 35 minutes or until casserole is puffed and pecans are toasted. Serve immediately.   *Makes 8 servings*

Nutrients per Serving:

Calories	203 (21% calories from fat)				
Total Fat	5 g	Carbohydrate	35 g	Iron	1 mg
Saturated Fat	1 g	Dietary Fiber	trace	Vitamin A	1923 RE
Cholesterol	trace	Protein	3 g	Vitamin C	19 mg
Sodium	202 mg	Calcium	48 mg	Sugar	1 g

DIETARY EXCHANGES: 2 Starch/Bread, 1½ Fat